Beautiful rainbow world

created by **Suzee Carlile-Ramirez** and **Lynne Carlile-Raspet**

original lyrics by **Daria Marmaluk-Hajioannou**

published by

two poppies

an imprint of Multicultural Kids, Inc.

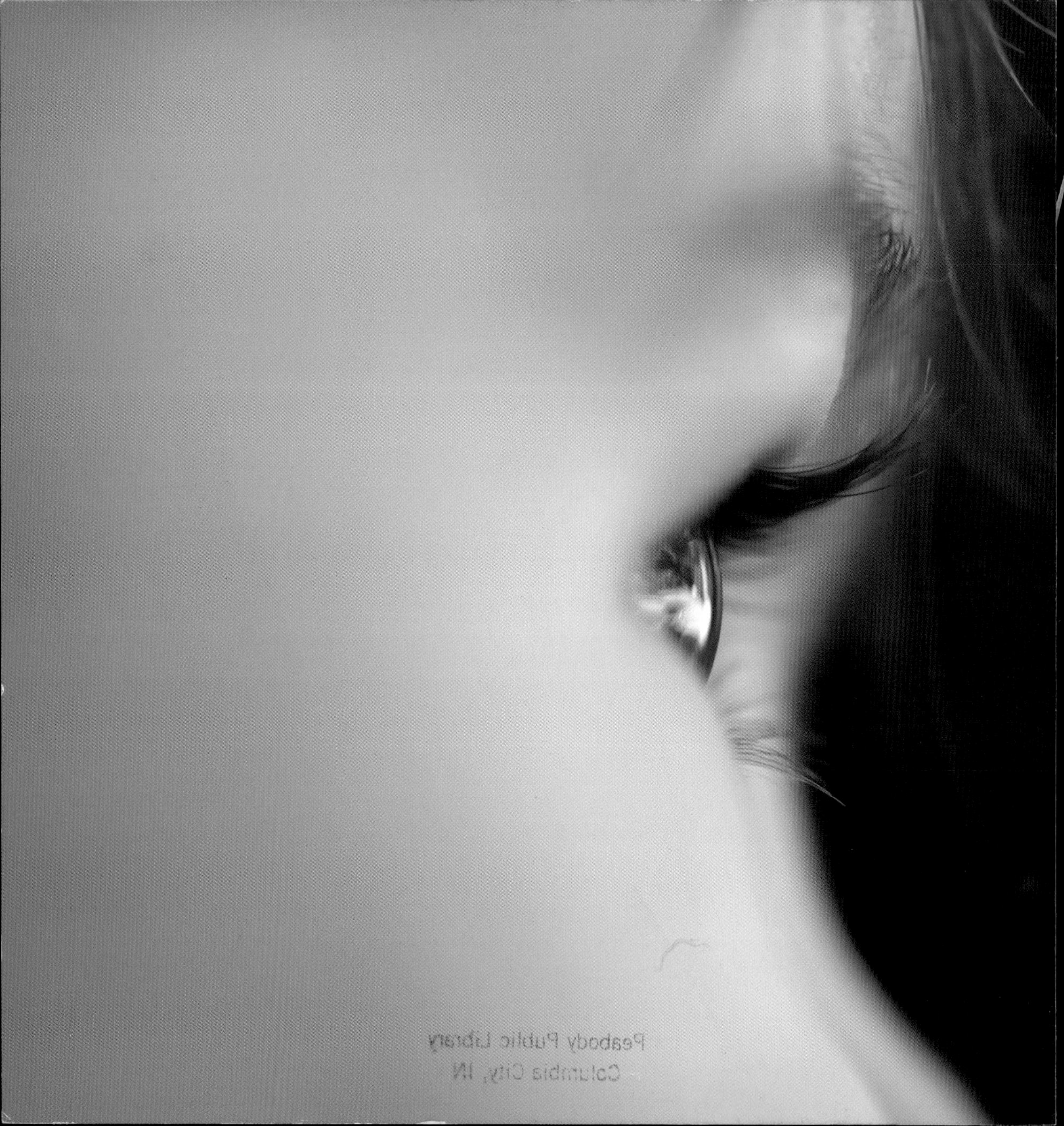

Today I woke up to see...

A beautiful rainbow world

Won't you dream it along with me?

A beautiful rainbow world

Beautiful rainbow, beautiful rainbow, beautiful rainbow, beautiful rainbow, beautiful rainbow, beautiful rainbow world... world...

Red, black, yellow...
...brown and white

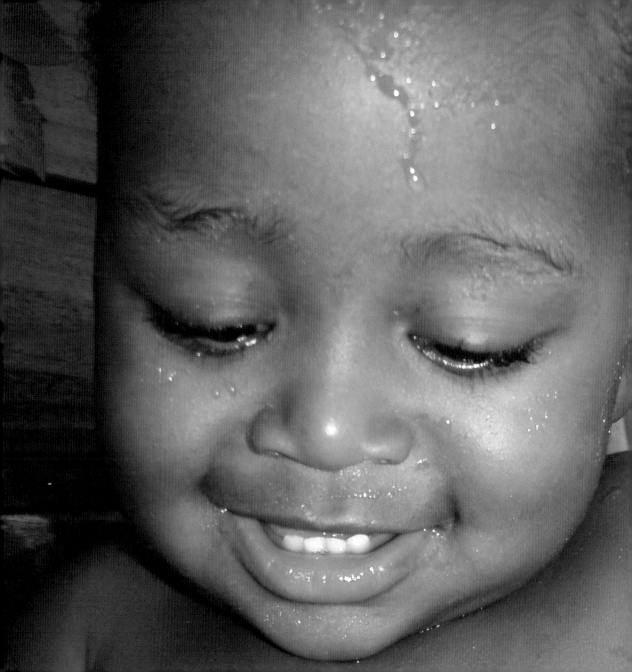

A beautiful rainbow world

Dancing together in the light

A beautiful rainbow world

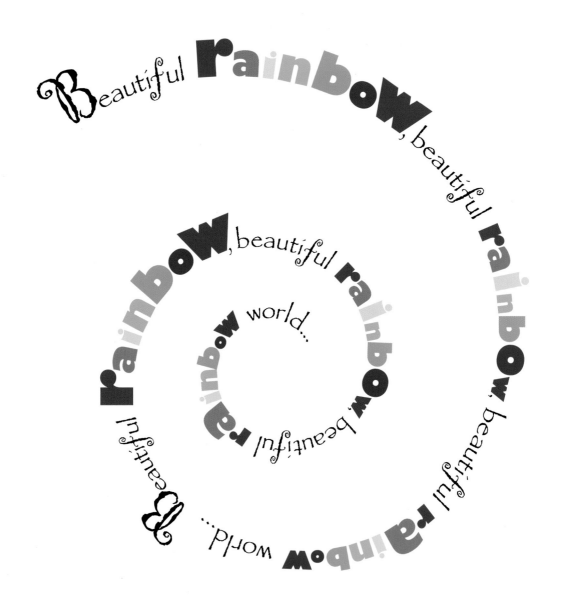

Beautiful rainbow, beautiful rainbow, beautiful rainbow, beautiful rainbow, beautiful rainbow, beautiful rainbow world... world...

22

No one lost or left behind

$\mathcal{A}$ beautiful rainbow world

Each one their own treasure finds

In this beautiful

rainbow world

Beautiful rainbow, beautiful rainbow, beautiful rainbow, beautiful rainbow, beautiful rainbow, beautiful rainbow, beautiful world... world... beautiful rainbow world...

*L*ooking through eyes
brown, green, or blue…

A beautiful rainbow world

And hair that's perfect
just for you!

A beautiful rainbow world

Beautiful rainbow, beautiful rainbow, beautiful rainbow, beautiful rainbow, beautiful rainbow, beautiful rainbow world... world... world...

*L*anguages and
customs all delight

A beautiful rainbow world

We're all so different,
yet so alike

A beautiful rainbow world

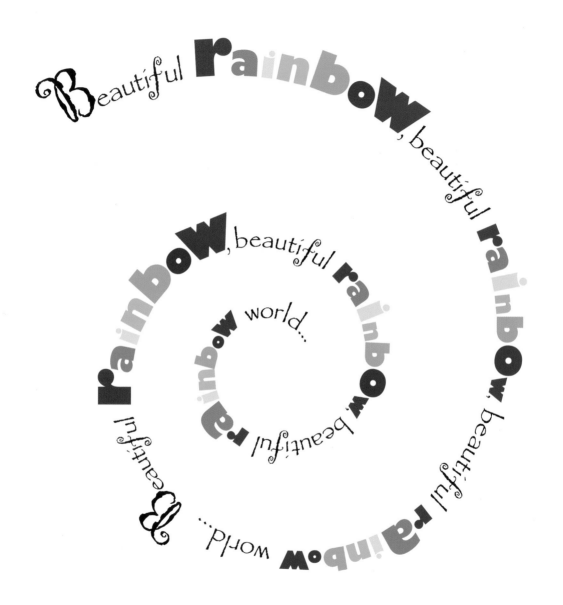

Beautiful rainbow, beautiful rainbow, beautiful rainbow, beautiful rainbow, beautiful rainbow world... world... beautiful rainbow, beautiful rainbow world...

Joyful laughter
as we play

$\mathcal{A}$ beautiful rainbow world

Hugging
and loving
every day

In this beautiful rainbow world

Beautiful rainbow, beautiful rainbow, beautiful rainbow, beautiful rainbow, beautiful rainbow, beautiful rainbow world... world...

contributing photographers

Ambrose, Tanzyn
ridgemeadowsphotography.com
British Columbia, Canada | cover photo, page 5

Anderson, Tom
kadphotography.com
California, United States | pages 24-25

Bardin, Changwen
California, United States | page 30

Bieber, Raphael
flickr.com/photos/raphy8
Rhode Island, United States | page 19

Dean, Changwei
cwdtd@yahoo.com
California, United States | Melbourne, Australia
pages 10, 12-13, 36-37, back

Just, Catherine
catherinejust.com
Utah, United States | page 59

Kellogg, Summer
summerkphotography.com
Ohio, United States | pages 48-49, 60-61, 78

Lee, Chiehwei
flickr.com/photos/maxcilla
Taipei, Taiwan | page 35

Lodha, Sahil
flickr.com/photos/simplysahil5
Maharashtra, India | pages 6-7, 9

Mayoff, Jason
jasonmayoff.com
Quebec, Canada | page 38

Novario, Meredith
meredithnovario.com
Okinaya, Japan | page 14

Raspet, Lynne
TwoPoppies.com
flickr.com/photos/lynneraspet
California, Georgia & Texas, United States
pages 20, 23, 33, 41, 42, 45, 54, 57, 62, 66-67, 71, 73, back

Ribes, Thomas
thomas.ribes@gmx.com
London, United Kingdom | pages 2-3

Robinson, Emily
emilyrobinsonphoto.com
Florida, United States | page 64

Rohidas, Lalit
lalit.rohidas@gmail.com
Odisha, India | page 46

Sampaio, Gina
New Jersey, United States | pages 16-17, 51

Saripova, Oksana
Saint-Petersburg, Russia | page 28, back

Shglila, Bashar
flickr.com/photos/bentaher
Tripoli, Libya | page 27

Studio E Photography | Wendy Ewing
studioe-photo.com
New Mexico, United States | page 69

Wick, Anne
thislittlesoul.com
Tours, France | page 75

Wilson, Sebrina
sebrinawilsonphotography.com
Ontario, Canada | page 53

All photos are copyrighted and are property of photographers.
Please contact the photographers directly for more information.

We dedicate this book
to our amazing children ~
Ellie, Paris, ZZ, Eva, Razzie and Gus

… and to all the children who are part of this
"Beautiful Rainbow World"

*We want to raise our children so that they
can take a sense of pleasure in both their
own heritage and the diversity of others.
~ Mister Rogers*

Suzee and Lynne are the two youngest sisters in a family of five children. Inspired by their own multicultural family (whose ancestry includes roots from Germany, Scotland, Ireland, Mexico, the Philippines, Portugal [Azores], Sweden, and Native America) ~ this book was dreamed up out of the beauty they saw not only in their own culturally mixed children, but children of all colors. This is their first book ~ with many more in the dream/creative stages of development.

Suzee Carlile Ramirez resides in Orange County, California with her husband, two lovely animal- and beach-loving girls (we'd have a farm on the ocean if they had their way!), and their rescued dogs and cat. She loves being active, creative, adventurous, and living with a sense of curiosity, awe, and wonder.

Lynne Carlile Raspet is a mom of four who bounces all over the country (especially the South) with her Air Force pilot hubby and loves discovering new places to adventure. Capturing real life with her camera including morning walks, road trips, and the baby squirrels they fostered (see page 41) is her idea of a good time. She believes in serendipity including an adorable kitty who appeared at midnight on Christmas Eve and became part of their family.

Daria Marmaluk-Hajioannou is an internationally known folksinger who for the last two decades has traveled the globe, learning, sharing and making music while building communities and encouraging a new view of hope and peace for all the world's children. In the United States, she has won national awards for her educational work as well as her children's music CDs including several Parents' Choice Awards, Creative Child, NAPPA Award (National Association for Parenting Publications), and a Children's Music Web Award.

Song Download: To download your copy of "Beautiful Rainbow World" by Daria, please go to **www.brwsong.com** and follow the instructions.

A portion of the earnings from this book will benefit organizations striving to better the lives of global children.

Note: Original lyrics of "Beautiful Rainbow World" by Daria A. Marmaluk-Hajioannou (through page 34). Lyrics were extended by Suzee Ramirez for usage in this book with permission and consultation of Daria.

ISBN 978-0-9915340-0-5
Preassigned Library of Congress Control Number: 2014936211

Copyright © 2014
Published by Two Poppies, an imprint of Multicultural Kids, Inc.

Book design by Suzee Ramirez

Production Date April 2014
Printed by WeSP Printer, Gyeonggi-do, South Korea
Job/Batch # 011314/40699-0

www.TwoPoppies.com | www.MulticulturalKids.com

we offer gratitude for our supporters

Abregov family
Ranita and Maniyah Anderson
Tiffanie Bacon and family
Toby Baldinger
Ballard family
Mike and Sher Berkus
Mary J. Branson
Abram, Karin, and Irene Burk
Cain family
Campbell family
Laura Curtis Cannon
Bobbie and John Carlile
Dan Carlile
David and Etelvina Carlile
Ann Carlile-Laycook
Sherry Christensen
Matthew and Sarah Cichowski
Creel family
Kathy and Dani Dawson

Dave, Wendy, Jake and Tiana Garcia
Valerie Goldsworthy
Steve and Rene Harwood
Heritage Preschool
bobi keenan
KidsAndCultures.com
Kochan family
Maria, David, and Natalia Lopez
Kai and Kala Lucas
McCall family
Suz McGill
Jan Morehead
Julie Norwood
Derik Olsson and Kate Manley
Ott family of Texas
Judy Owens
Pauly family
Lacey and Clay Quinby
Quintanar family

Mark Rasdorf
Vann and Kathy Riley
Maria Rivas
Rogers family
Chad, Erin and Jameson Rudolph
Melissa Sadikoff
Greg and Shirley Schmidt
Greg Schmidt and Shauna Carroll
Jason Schmidt
Sophie Sebrow
Doris Shen
Stevens family
Stock family
Sunlight Christian Academy
Vander Broek family
Teresa Vitelli
Bart and Amanda Ward
Wahl family
Sheri and Willy Workman

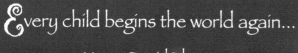

Every child begins the world again...

~ Henry David Thoreau